Word Search Puzzles

PUZZLED about GOD?

REPRODUCIBLE

by Theresa C. Hayes

STANDARD PUBLISHING
Cincinnati, Ohio

If you love word search puzzles, perhaps you've already discovered that the easiest way to solve them is with highlighter pens. This is much neater than drawing circles, and makes it much easier to find your unused letters. In these puzzles, you will be looking for all the words in **bold face type.** Be careful, there are some words (accidently!) in the puzzles that are not in the stories—and if you select them you may mess up your hidden messages. The words are hidden in every direction and the puzzles are very tightly woven. Search carefully!

The Standard Publishing Company, Cincinnati, Ohio
A division of Standex International Corporation

© 1997 by The Standard Publishing Company
All rights reserved
Printed in the United States of America

04 03 02 01 00 99 98 97   5 4 3 2 1

ISBN 0-7847-0639-5

Contents

God Is the Creator
In the **beginning God created** the **heavens** and the **earth** (Genesis 1:1). **God created man** in his **own image**, . . . **male** and **female** he **created** them (1:27).

God Is the One Who Is
God said to Moses, "I am who I am. This is **what you** are to **say** to the **Israelites: I AM** has sent me to you."

Exodus 3:14

God Is the Beginning and the End
"I am the **Alpha** and the **Omega**," says the **Lord God**, "**who** is, and who **was**, and who is to **come**, the **Almighty**."

Revelation 1:8

(Alpha is the first letter of the Greek alphabet and Omega is the last.)

God Is Unequaled
I am **he**, I am **he who** will **sustain you**.
I have **made** you and I **will carry** you;
I will **sustain** you and I will **rescue** you.
To whom will you **compare** me or **count** me **equal**?

Isaiah 46:4, 5

God Is Our Heavenly Father
"**Our Father** in **heaven**, **hallowed** be your **name**."

Matthew 6:9

For you did not **receive** a spirit that **makes** you a **slave** **again** to **fear**, but you received the Spirit of **sonship**. And by him we **cry**, "*Abba* (Daddy), **Father**." The **Spirit himself** **testifies** with **our** spirit that we are God's **children**.

Romans 8:15, 16

Word Search

```
E I O   H F E
M U M Y N E L R
O S C A A A E E
C U R S M V S H
O S E O E E E M T
P T A   N I A
I A T   S H F
H I E   E O N
S N D   L C I
N O C   A R A
O H O   M E T
S W U   W A S
I H N   I T U
A A T   L E S
M T O   L D O

E H E A V E N G
A B B A G O D N
R R E H T A F I
T S W   O I N
H L H   I S N
D A O   S E I
E V U R O R I G
T E E O D A F E
A O V L Y E I B
E A I   L T S
R H E   I S P
C P C   T E I
D L E   E T R
O A R   S U I
G O D   O O T

O C O H F
M A K E S
C R A D O
R H E
Y Y W
O T O
U H L
E G L
R I A
A M H
P L O
M A E
O O U D R
O C Q A U
A G E M O
```

Evidence of God

Some people say, "If God exists, why doesn't He show himself to me?" God's answer is all around:

Since the **creation** of the **world God's invisible qualities**—**his** eternal **power** and **divine nature**—**have been clearly seen, being understood from** what has **been made**, so that **men** are **without excuse**.

Romans 1:20

The **heavens declare** the **glory** of **God**; the **skies proclaim** the **work** of his **hands. Day** after day they **pour forth speech; night** after **night** they **display knowledge. There** is no speech or **language where** their **voice** is **not** heard.

Psalm 19:1-4

We are **bringing** you **good news**, telling you to turn from these **worthless things** to the **living God, who** made **heaven** and **earth** and **sea** and **everything** in them. In the **past**, he **let all nations** go **their own way**. Yet he has **not** left himself **without testimony**: He has **shown kindness** by **giving** you **rain** from **heaven** and **crops** in their seasons; he **provides you** with **plenty** of **food** and **fills your hearts** with **joy**.

Acts 14:15-17

```
            C W H O Q S
          R S O S U D E T
        O D G R A O L H O N T
      P N N N L G B E N W H Y D
    S A A O I D I R N O S T O T
    H E T T V S E M H I Y O U E
  H D S I A I S E S N T G N R S H
  E I E N V L E T C E A D H A T E
  A S K N O W L E D G E T F T I A
  V P I R I O H R E R R N I U M V
  E L N W C R T U S I C M L O O E
  N A E Y E K R T T K R A L H N N
  G Y V L M E O A D H I D S T Y S
  N R A R V O W N E N E E B I D K
  I E E A D M R O C D H S S W I E
  G W H E R E U F L O T W T N V A
  N O E L A N G U A G E E D E I R
  I P H C E E P S R A I N O E N T
  R G N I H T Y R E V E X G B E H
  B E I N G E C H T S A P I Y O J
  D O O F G X A T S E D I V O R P
    M I A L C O R P T H G I N U
      D P O U R O T P L E N T Y
      A R S S F E S I H G A
        Y E T U O H T I W
          S G N I H T
```

__ __   __ __ __ __   __ __ __ __   __ __ __

__ __ __ __ __ __ __   __ __ __ __ __ __ __

If you have solved the puzzle correctly, the unused letters
will fit into these blanks to spell out a message.

God's Strength, Our Strength

Acknowledging God as our heavenly Father and accepting Jesus Christ as our personal Savior brings blessings almost too numerous to list. Certainly one of the most exciting is the gift of God's own Holy Spirit.

What does the presence of God's Spirit in our lives do for us? He allows us to share in God's power. With this power, we can resist temptations, we can find courage to take a stand for God, we can have the strength to face all our daily battles. How incredible that God would share His strength with us!

Jesus looked at **them** and **said**, "**With man** this is **impossible**, but with **God all things** are **possible**."
Matthew 19:26

I **can do everything through him who gives** me **strength**.
Philippians 4:13

The **sting** of **death** is **sin**, and the **power** of **sin** is the **law**. But **thanks** be to **God**! He **gives** us the **victory through** our **Lord Jesus Christ**.
1 Corinthians 15:56, 57

But I **call** to **God**, and the **Lord saves** me. **Evening, morning** and **noon** I **cry out** in **distress**, and he **hears** my **voice**. He **ransoms** me **unharmed** from the **battle waged against** me, **even though many oppose** me.
Psalm 55:16, 17

So do **not fear**, for I am with **you**;
    do not be **dismayed**, for I am **your God**.
I **will strengthen you** and **help** you;
    I **will uphold** you **with** my **righteous right hand**.

Isaiah 41:10

```
T  S  T  U  P  H  O  L  D  W  C  A  L  L  S
H  G  S  E  L  V  B  G  N  I  N  R  O  M  I
G  N  I  N  E  V  E  A  L  L  A  W  O  T  N
I  I  R  M  H  T  I  W  T  L  G  S  K  H  E
R  H  H  A  P  Y  N  C  W  T  N  O  E  R  P
U  T  C  N  L  O  R  D  T  A  L  R  D  O  Y
N  O  T  Y  O  U  S  T  R  O  G  E  W  U  H
H  T  G  N  E  R  T  S  H  N  R  E  I  G  G
A  T  S  S  E  R  T  S  I  D  R  Y  D  H  U
R  N  S  I  G  H  E  H  C  B  D  O  I  G  O
M  H  A  N  D  V  T  T  H  R  L  U  S  N  H
E  I  A  O  I  Y  U  G  O  D  Y  E  M  I  T
D  M  G  G  R  A  B  L  N  R  H  S  A  T  D
S  U  O  E  T  H  G  I  R  E  E  O  Y  S  E
U  D  V  O  I  C  E  A  A  V  R  A  E  F  A
J  E  S  U  S  A  G  R  A  O  U  T  D  S  T
S  V  U  W  H  N  S  S  O  P  P  O  S  E  H
A  E  S  I  W  H  O  S  K  N  A  H  T  V  H
I  N  E  L  B  I  S  S  O  P  I  H  T  I  W
D  M  J  L  T  H  E  M  T  H  R  O  U  G  H
```

_ _ _ _ _ _ _ _ _   _ _ _ _ _ _ _

_ _ _

9

Love Defined

First Corinthians 13 is often referred to as the "Love Chapter" of the Bible because it beautifully defines love. How many of the bold-faced words can you find in the heart?

Love is **patient, love** is **kind**. It **does not envy**, it **does not boast**, it is **not proud**. It is **not rude**, it is **not self-seeking**, it is **not easily angered**, it **keeps** no **record** of **wrongs**. Love does **not delight** in **evil** but **rejoices** with the **truth**. It always **protects, always trusts, always** hopes, **always perseveres. Love never fails.**

1 Corinthians 13:4-8

For another lovely message, fill in the blanks with the unused letters.

```
        D L A              Y R N
      D N O O W          V E L T H
    T T E V E S E      N J T O H R K
  E H R E E V S R E  E O M R V L A E D
  I G U N F I P N O T I N E A E O I E T
  T I S H K L E H O C O C D O P V R P R
  S L T E I A R N E T O N U P N E S S U
  D E S L N O S S V R B E R B G Y U A T
  P D L T D E E T D H E O G N A R L N H
  R E F O A V T E S U T A W O W E A
    O D S F E E F D T T L S A I L
    T H E R A R A O A G Y T W
      E E E S S N I N S A A
      C S K E I O L P Y
      T I I R L S S
      S W N L Y
      O V G
      E
```

___ ___ ____ ____

_____: _____ ___,

___ ____. ___ ___

_____ __ _____ __

____.

1 Corinthians 13:13

Finding Your Way in the Old Testament

The Old Testament is the history of the **world** from the time of creation through the prophecies of the coming Messiah. The first seventeen books of **history** record the rise and fall of the Hebrew nation. Genesis, as its name implies, records the beginning of the world, the first destruction of the world (the flood), and the generations of man up to Jacob. Exodus records the four hundred years of Hebrew slavery, their exodus from **Egypt**, and the giving of the Ten Commandments. Leviticus is a book of (more) laws. Numbers and Deuteronomy record the forty years in the wilderness and contain **more** laws. These five books are called the books of **law**.

The next twelve books record the conquest of Canaan (the promised land) and the **rise** and **fall** of the Hebrew people as they turned to and from God again and **again**. In these books you will find the record of David's **life**.

Job through the Song of Songs are **poetry** books, although we **lose** much of the form in the English translation. Job deals with suffering and man's relationship to God. Most of the psalms (songs) were written by **David**. Proverbs, Ecclesiastes, and Song of Songs were written by David's son, Solomon.

The last seventeen books are **prophecy**. The prophets Isaiah, Jeremiah, Daniel, Hosea, etc. revealed future events with absolute accuracy—because their knowledge came from God. History books record the perfect fulfillment of some prophecies, and Jesus Christ fulfilled **every** prophecy regarding the coming **Messiah**. Every prophecy as yet unfulfilled concerns the future.

Genesis
Exodus
Leviticus
Numbers
Deuteronomy
Joshua
Judges
Ruth
First & Second
Samuel
First Kings
Second Kings
First & Second
Chronicles
Ezra
Nehemiah
Esther
Job
Psalms
Proverbs
Ecclesiastes
Song of Songs
Isaiah
Jeremiah
Lamentations
Ezekiel
Daniel
Hosea
Joel
Amos
Obadiah
Jonah
Micah
Nahum
Habakkuk

Zephaniah   Zechariah
Haggai   Malachi

```
L A M E N T A T I O N S
E H A E N L P R U T H E
I C A F D U E S O L A G
N P C I H H M R A A C D
A W V L S O A B I L I U
D A M E E S E I E S M J
D L R O W S E V A R E S
G A J P T A I M M S S E
J E O H O T U A O L I X
E Z E K I E L P S S Y O
R R L C L H T A B T C D
E A U A E V E R Y K E U
M S I S E N E G Y U H S
I M O R E V N I T K P E
A H A N O J A E A K O L
H I A R G G R U D A R C
H S P I G O H O M B P I
A T E A N S F A G A I N
I O H O O A E S O H K O
D R M J L G H J O B I R
A Y U L E G Y P T N N H
B A H A I M E H E N G C
O H A I R A H C E Z S S
K I N G S I H C A L A M
```

Finding Your Way in the New Testament

Like the Old Testament, the New begins with five books of **history**. The first four are called the **Gospels**, and they record the life of **Jesus**. The fifth book records the acts of the early church.

The apostles (one sent on a mission) Matthew, Mark, Luke, and John, each give accounts of many of the things Jesus said and did, although their books do not completely overlap. Reading these four Gospels gives us a very complete and accurate picture of Jesus.

Acts, written by the apostle **Paul**, records the formation of the **church** and spread of the message of the church to **Gentiles** (those who are not Jews). The book also contains the record of Paul's life from the time as a dedicated Jew named Saul he persecuted the Christians, through his conversion and thirty-five years missionary work, until he was finally beheaded in Rome because of his faith.

The next twenty-one books are called the **Epistles** (letters). First and Second Timothy and Philemon are letters from Paul to those men. The other letters are either named for the churches who received them (in Rome, Corinth, Galatia, Ephesus, etc.), or for their authors.

These letters were intended to be circulated among the churches "for the edification of the **saints**." Today, we receive from them the same edifiction that our earliest Christians brothers and sisters received.

Revelation is exactly what its name implies, the revelation of what is to come: the return of Jesus Christ and the end of this world.

Matthew
Mark
Luke
John
Acts

Romans
First
  Corinthians
Second
  Corinthians
Galatians
Ephesians
Philippians
Colossians
First
  Thessalonians
Second
  Thessalonians
First
  Timothy
Second
  Timothy
Titus
Philemon

Hebrews
James
First **Peter**
Second **Peter**
First **John**
Second **John**
Third **John**
Jude

Revelation

```
P T H E B R E W S W H O
E H V E R S L E P S O G
H E I E A R N H O J S E
M S L L Y T I T U S D W
O S U T I L R T D U A Y
E A K I E P N A J N H D
P L E M P G P M O T B T
H O O O I A E I O L R S
E N I T S L T M A E J R
S I E H T A I V T N E I
I A E Y L T S E H T S F
A N H E E I P I E M U W
N S V H S A O P S S S E
S E N S T N I A S N T C
R O M A N S K R A M M O
E J H G E N T I L E S L
Y R O T S I H J O H N O
A S E H T T E A N R F S
S E C O N D D M I N I S
T S R I F A R E A L R I
H C R U H C I S N C S A
J O H N L I H F S E T N
C C O R I N T H I A N S
```

_ _ _ _ _ _ _ _ _   _ _ _ _

_ _   _ _ _ _   _ _ _

_ _ _ _ _ _ _   _ _ _ _

_ _ _   _ _ _ _ _   _ _   _ _ _

_ _ _ _ _ _ _   _ _ _ _ _.

John 5:24

Not Just Words on Paper

When God gave us His written Word, He gave us all that we need to learn of Him and grow into a relationship of faith with Him.

First, God's Word works to convince unbelievers of their need for God: "All **over** the **world** this **gospel** is bearing **fruit** and **growing**, just as it has been **doing among** you **since** the day you **heard** it and **understood** God's **grace** in all its **truth**" (Colossians 1:6).

How do the Scriptures do this? "The word of **God** is **living** and **active. Sharper** than **any double-edged sword**, it **penetrates** even to **dividing soul** and spirit, **joints** and **marrow**; it **judges** the **thoughts** and **attitudes** of the **heart. Nothing** in all **creation** is **hidden** from God's **sight. Everything** is **uncovered** and laid **bare** before the **eyes** of **him** to whom we **must** give **account**" (Hebrews 4:12, 13).

How can a book change lives? "All **Scripture** is **God-breathed** [inspired] and is **useful** for **teaching, rebuking, correcting** and **training** in **righteousness**" (2 Timothy 3:16).

God himself promises that "As the **rain** and the **snow come** down from **heaven**, and do **not** return to it without **watering** the **earth** and **making** it **bud** and **flourish** . . . so is my **word** that **goes out** from my mouth: It will not return to me **empty, but** will **accomplish** what I **desire** and **achieve** the **purpose** for which I **sent** it" (Isaiah 55:10, 11).

Finally, the Bible is absolutely essential to life because, "Man **does not live** on **bread alone, but** on **every word** that comes **from** the **mouth** of **God**" (Matthew 4:4).

```
P Y T M M G S E A R T H G D W
U D U O A N T O T U S N O R O
R E B U K I N G T R I N S O R
P R W T I H I L I H G O P W R
O E D H N C O U T E H I E A A
S V O O G A J O U A T T L L M
E O R R O E N S D V S A D O G
S C R I P T U R E E E E D N R
T N E S G S S Y S N G R A E O
S U B N E H E R I D D C N S W
E U O F S S T R E B U D Y A I
T M U L T B R E A D J I G A N
A L G A H H L P O M N O O C G
R I G C G B T R F U E U D T O
T V N C U A R A G S S E B I E
E E I O O R H H R T M N R V C
N M D M H E T S A O Y T E E N
E T I P T N U O C C A I A S I
P R V L P T R A E H H U T D S
D A I I N O T O N C H R H O N
O I D S A M I H A T S F E I O
G N I H T Y R E V E I N D N W
H I D D E N W A T E R I N G O
G N I T C E R R O C U A H P R
S G N I V I L D V W O R D A L
E V E R Y T P M E L L S E O D
S W O R D E S I R E F R O M M
```

__ __ __ __   __ __ __ __   __ __ . . . __   __ __ __ __ __

__ __ __ __   __ __   __ __ __ __ __ .   __ __ __ __ __   119:105

Names of Jesus

Seven hundred years before **Jesus** was born, the **prophet Isaiah** told of the **virgin** who would give birth to a **son**, and call him Immanuel (7:14). **Immanuel means "God with us."** Later, **Isaiah** revealed many more names and qualities:

For to us a **child** is **born**, to us a **son** is given, and the **government** will be on his **shoulders**.

And he will be called **Wonderful Counselor, Mighty God, Everlasting Father, Prince of Peace**.

Of the increase of **his** government and **peace** there will be no **end**.

Isaiah 9:6, 7

In the book of John, **Jesus** gives himself names that explain His **character** and His **purpose**. He said, "I am the **bread of life**. He who comes to me will **never** go **hungry**, and he who **believes** in me will **never** be **thirsty**" (6:35). "I am the **light of the world**" (9:5). "I am the **gate**; whoever **enters** through me will be **saved** (10:9). "I am the **resurrection** and the **life**. He who **believes** in me will live, even though he **dies**; and **whoever** lives and **believes** in me will **never die**" (11:25). "I am the **way** and the **truth** and the **life**. No one **comes** to the **Father** except **through** me" (14:6).

"I am the **true vine**, and my **Father** is the **gardener**. He **cuts** off every **branch** in me that **bears** no **fruit**, while every **branch** that does **bear** fruit he **prunes** so that it **will** be even more **fruitful**. . . . **Remain** in me, and I will **remain** in you. No **branch** can **bear** fruit by itself; it **must remain** in the **vine**. . . . I am the **vine**; you are the **branches**" (15:1-5).

```
E P E R E N E D R A G S S V E S
N R S R E D L U O H S O R P R U
T O O S E V E I L E B N A E Y S
E P N P R I N C E O F P E A C E
R H R E V E N O S T N E B C H J
S E W D N E V E N E V E R E I H
U T O L E C I E U T S U M A L D
H E T R V D M C O M E S E L D E
T F R O E N F L C H N I A M E R
I I U W R S R B L F W B N S S D
W L E E L T U O U A O R S V O N
D F V H A U I R F T N A I T P U
O O I T S C T N R H V N D H R H
G D N F T Y F I E E E C I R U N
E A E O I R U A D R C H E N P E
B E A T N G L M N M E T V O F V
E R B H G N L E O T C I I P D E
L B R G F U I R W A N H R O E S
I S A I A H W G R E L U G T N B
E S N L T B E A R O N Y I H I E
V E C R H D H T Y E T W N R A A
E V H E E C I E S H F E H O M R
S E F F R U I T G L A F C U E F
H I S Y T S R I H T T I N G R R
L L E U N A M M I L H L A H B U
J E S U S H T U R T E E R S S I
A B R A N C H E S V R E B D I T
```

_ _ _ _ _ _ _ _ _ _ _ _ _ _

_ _ _ _ _ _ _ _ _ _ _ _ _ _

_ _ _ _ _ _ _ _ _ _ _ _ _ _ —.

Acts 2:21

19

God's Willingness to Save

But I **call** to **God**, and the **Lord saves** me.
Evening, **morning** and **noon** I **cry out** in **distress**,
   and he **hears** my **voice**.
He **ransoms** me unharmed from the **battle waged against**
    me,
   even though **many oppose** me.
God, who is **enthroned forever**,
   will **hear them** and **afflict** them. . . .
Cast your cares on the **Lord** and he will **sustain** you;
   he will **never** let the **righteous** fall.

Psalm 55:16-19, 22

You see, at just the **right time**, when we were **still
powerless**, **Christ** died for the **ungodly**. . . . **God
demonstrates** his **own love** for us in this: While we were still
sinners, **Christ died** for us.

   Since we have **now** been **justified** by his **blood**, how
much more shall we be **saved** from **God's wrath through**
him! For if, when we **were God's** enemies, we were
reconciled to him **through** the **death** of his **Son**, how **much
more, having been reconciled**, shall we be **saved through**
his **life**!

Paul, in Romans 5:6-10

For the **wages** of sin is **death**, but the **gift** of **God** is **eternal
life** in **Christ Jesus our Lord**.

Paul, in Romans 6:23

For my **Father's** will is that **everyone** who **looks** to the
Son and **believes** in **him** shall **have eternal** life, and I will
raise him up at the last day.

Jesus, in John 6:40

```
Y L D O G N U G O D T S A C G
H N E V E F O R E V E R R H O
G I A S A V E D M T U A S R D
U H F E T H E M A O E E I I S
O A F N Y O U R N H F R N S T
R V L T O U T H Y A I O N T I
H E I H E S O P P O L M E A L
T V C R N G S M O S N A R E L
L I T O C O D I S T R E S S E
O O M N N D H S D G O D S F W
R E R E O C E E L O V E I M A
D E C D U V I S H A L L T H G
E T H M A F I L C R Y I A N E
V H R S I N S S E R A C I I S
A R I T C S U W H D T N H A H
S O S E R V O I C E R O T T G
T U T A C P E H U O G C A S U
J G E E H Y T M M A O E E U O
E H H S R E H T A F D R D S R
S Y A E I H G O D N O O N O H
U A V V S A I H I M O E V N T
S E I E T E R N A L L O R D L
K G N I N E V E R T B D L E L
O I G L R I G H T S N I A G A
O F I E F H T A R W O E E A C
L T W B U T B E E N W D N W O
```

— — — — —   — — — — —   — — — — —

— — — —   — — —   — — — — —   — — — —.

John 10:10

But I'm Not a Bad Person

Many people believe they will spend eternity with God because they have never murdered, or committed adultery, or robbed anyone. They are saying that they "abide by the law." In the passage below, Paul points out that *no one* is able to live without ever breaking a law—especially the law of God. In fact, the more we know the law, and the more we know the character of God, the more we realize how sinful we are! Who among us has never "murdered" someone's spirit with a hateful verbal attack? Who has never indulged in sexual banter (and fantasies) with someone who was not ours? Who has never stolen time from work, lying to the boss in the process? The good news is that we are made righteous (forgiven) even though we cannot keep the law. This is what Jesus has done for us. Paul writes that just as *all* have sinned, *all* may be forgiven.

Now we **know** that **whatever** the **law says**, it says to **those** who are **under** the **law**, so that **every mouth may** be **silenced** and the **whole world held accountable** to **God. Therefore** no **one will** be **declared righteous** in **his sight** by **observing** the **law; rather**, through the **law** we **become conscious** of **sin.**

But now a **righteousness** from **God, apart from law**, has been **made known**. . . . This **righteousness from God comes through faith** in **Jesus Christ** to **all** who **believe**. There is no **difference**, for all **have sinned** and **fall short** of the **glory** of **God**, and are **justified freely** by his **grace through** the **redemption** that **came** by **Christ Jesus.**

Romans 3:19-24

```
C H R I S T S N W O N K A A G
A F A I T H H Y O O H E L D O
M O R F G L O R N Y R O L G D
E M O U T H R E K O D L L C C
Y L E E R F T V F J E A D H O
L D E R A L C E D E N W I R N
L O J W A L R H O S N D F I S
A G U H A E W B S U I E F S C
F E S A H A S R U S S C E T I
T L T T L E V I S W O N R H O
H B I E R A W G E T S E E I U
R A F V E E W H J U A L N S S
O T I E S S D T O B Y I C B S
U N E R E O N E L L S S E E E
G U D M G T T O M A E I R C L
H O O N R H Y U N P W A A O L
A C G A G A E S O H T R E M I
V C P I M A D E T H G I S E W
E A R D B E L I E V E M O R F
W O N H G U O R H T R E D N U
```

___ ____ _____.

The Parable of the Sower

Jesus sometimes taught in parables because He knew that those listeners who were honestly searching for God would understand, while those who were there to mock or criticize would hear only riddles. The same is true today.

This is how Jesus explained "The Parable of the Sower." (Found in Matthew 13:3-9.)

When **anyone** hears the **message about** the **kingdom** and **does** not **understand** it, the evil **one comes** and **snatches away** what **was sown** in his **heart**. This is the **seed sown along** the **path**. The **one** who received the **seed** that fell on **rocky places** is the **man** who hears the **word** and at **once receives** it with **joy**. **But since** he **has** no **root**, he **lasts only** a **short** time. **When trouble** or **persecution comes because** of the **word**, he **quickly falls** away. The one who received the **seed that** fell **among** the **thorns** is the **man** who **hears** the **word**, but the **worries** of this **life** and the **deceitfulness** of **wealth choke** it, **making** it **unfruitful**. But the **one who** received the **seed** that fell on **good soil** is the **man** who **hears** the **word** and **understands** it. He **produces** a **crop, yielding** a **hundred, sixty** or **thirty times what was sown**.

Matthew 13:19-23

Is your heart hard, like a beaten path? Or shallow like rocky soil? Or full of thorns (past hurts, worries, desires that are more important to you than God)? The Good News cannot take root and grow in hearts like these. But if your heart is like a rich, workable garden, God can produce a crop of faith, peace, joy, love, hope, patience, kindness, self-control— a bountiful crop that far exceeds your expectations!

24

```
Q U I C K L Y E C N O S E E D
N R N O N E O O S O D T H A T
W O R D O O J E O N F A L L S
O C O M E S I H A S B T W O O
S K H E A R S T O O R S A N W
O Y D O R O S S U A E O S G N
S E M O C R E T E C S S T T G
M S W H E N E H A E E T H A N
O A O D W S D L M N D S O H O
L W N O O H P I L G D A R W M
I U S R O O T U N E E L N E A
F G F H N R F I R Y E O S A P
E N W T E T K D T M S S Y L R
K I S S I A N R A R A T E T O
I D O E M U I N A G X N W H D
N L C V H H R E E I O W O O U
G E R I T C H F S Y S O R C C
D I O E P A T H N W O R D H E
O Y P C Y A W A O U I D O O S
M A N E C N I S N Y L N O K O
B U T R O U B L E S U A C E B
```

Be Wise to Deception

See to it that no one **takes** you **captive** through **hollow** and **deceptive philosophy**, which **depends** on **human tradition** and the basic **principles** of this **world** rather than on **Christ**.

Colossians 2:8

If anyone **teaches false doctrines** and does not **agree** to the **sound instruction** of our **Lord Jesus Christ** and to **godly** teaching, he is **conceited** and **understands nothing**. He has an **unhealthy** interest in **controversies** and **quarrels about words** that result in **envy,** strife, **malicious** talk, **evil suspicions** and **constant** friction between **men** of **corrupt mind,** who have **been robbed** of the **truth** and who **think** that **godliness** is a means to **financial gain**.

1 Timothy 6:3-5

But if you **harbor bitter envy** and **selfish ambition** in **your hearts,** do not **boast** about it or deny the **truth**. Such "**wisdom**" does not come **down** from **heaven** but is **earthly, unspiritual,** of the devil. For where you have **envy** and self-ish **ambition,** there you find **disorder** and every **evil practice**.

James 3:14-16

The light **shines** in the **darkness,** but the **darkness** has not **understood** it.

John 1:5

The **god** of this **age** [Satan] has **blinded** the minds of **unbelievers,** so that they **cannot see** the light of the **gospel** of the **glory** of **Christ,** who is the **image** of **God**.

2 Corinthians 4:4

```
L A I C N A N I F G O D L Y O O
N M O G O D L I N E S S H V K O
E B D E D N I L B O O P E N V Y
V I O E E T D L R O W I E H N
A T O V B E R R O S H H S T O I
E I S I B B A O O T T O L I N D
H O L L O W D L U V U A T S J A
O N E A R C I R S N E I T E G R
E Y R B O H T O D H B R S L O K
C L R O P R I O N M U U S P D N
I H A U E I O U A C S O L I V E
T T U T S S N O T H I N G C E S
C R Q M L T R I S D E P E N D S
A A E S A U O C R G T D B I T M
R E E D F N B H E L R E O R A I
P C S R O S R R D O U C A P K N
Y O R O D P A I N R T E S O E D
V N E W D I H S U Y H P T O S O
N S V S E R S T R E T T I B U O
E T E E T I D O C T R I N E S T
G A I N I T S I R H C V A E P S
A N L I E U N W O D O E G U I R
M T E H C A P T I V E A R D C E
I E B S N L E P S O G R E O I D
C A N N O T W I S D O M E G O N
Y O U R C S U O I C I L A M N U
D A R K N E S S H S I F L E S O
```

What's Up With Satan?

Many people today doubt that Satan exists. They consider themselves too sophisticated to believe in such a bizarre old story. And that suits Satan just fine. After all, his goal to destroy us will be much easier to accomplish if we don't recognize his plan or even **suspect** that he exists. But certainly no **one can** deny the existence of evil in this world—the evidence is all around us. What is the source of this evil?

The Bible speaks of **Satan** as **real**. **God** would not **warn** us about something that does **not** exist. Satan's **work** is to **separate** us from God. His **weapon** is to distort the truth of God—and get us to **believe** his lies. The Bible says that "**When** he **lies**, he **speaks his native language**, for he is a **liar** and the **father** of **lies**" (John 8:44). He has been extremely successful in getting the **world** to reject **God's** offer of **love** and **forgiveness** and **accept** instead the lies that we can take care of **ourselves**, that we don't **need** forgiveness, and we don't **need** God. Such **pride** and **self-centeredness** is the **root** of **every evil act**.

Peter warns us to "be **self-controlled** and **alert**. **Your enemy** the **devil prowls around** like a **roaring lion looking** for **someone** to **devour**" (1 Peter 5:8).

"**Put** on the **full armor** of **God** so that **you can take your stand against** the **devil's schemes**. For our **struggle** is **not against flesh** and **blood**, but against the . . . **powers** of this **dark world** and **against** the **spiritual forces** of **evil**" (Ephesians 6:11, 12).

Satan is **real** and **his power** is **great**, but if you are a **child** of **God**, "the **one who** is in **you** [God's Holy Spirit] is **greater than** the **one who** is in the **world**" (1 John 4:4).

```
W O R L D N U O R A S A L I A R
Y O U R E A L Y D N S K A E P S
E V E I L E B O C A N R U R T G
T A F E L G G U R T S A T U F R
A B L O O D H I S A D D I O N E
R R E N R A C T E S E N R V O A
A E S E T G H L L L V G I E T T
P H H E N A I I F O I O P D S S
E T G D O I L V C V L D S E E I
S A N L C N D E E E D E V I L S
S F I R F S T N N R L L K A N
R H R O L T E O T P E T E R N R
E N A W E S A I E S A S E O G A
W H O S S U R L R A L O S W U W
O R R P U S M U E T P E C C A L
P O T L A P O R D A C W H O G I
W O R L D E R M N N Y M E N E E
N T E U G C W T E Y C R M E P S
H I S F O T S A S O A S E O U E
S T A N D N F K S U N R S V T C
W R P R I D E E N G R E A T E R
H E E A G A I N S T U W V H V O
E L G O D S G N I K O O L A I F
N A T I V E W A R N Y P I N L L
```

— — — —   — —   — — —

— — — — —   — —   — — — —.

Who Needs Discipline?

Most adults do not think of themselves as needing discipline—at least, not like children do. But in the eyes of God, we are all children. And like any loving parent, God disciplines us.

The author of Hebrews (probably Paul) wrote quite a bit about discipline. First he quoted Proverbs 3:11, 12, and then he added his own comments:

"My **son**, do **not make light** of the **Lord's discipline**, and do **not lose heart** when he **rebukes you, because** the **Lord disciplines** those he **loves**, and he **punishes everyone** he **accepts** as a **son**."

Endure hardship as **discipline; God** is **treating you** as **sons**. For **what son** is not disciplined by **his father**? If you **are** not **disciplined** (and **everyone undergoes discipline**), **then you are illegitimate children** and not **true sons. Moreover**, we **have** all had **human fathers** who **disciplined** us and we **respected them** for it. **How much** more **should** we **submit** to the **Father** of **our spirits** and **live! Our fathers** disciplined us for a **little** while as they **thought best;** but **God disciplines** us for **our good**, that we **may share** in his **holiness**. No discipline seems **pleasant** at the **time,** but **painful**. Later on, **however,** it **produces** a **harvest** of **righteousness** and **peace** for **those who** have **been trained** by it.

Hebrews 12:5-11

```
R Y O U S S E N I L O H G F N
E N I L P I C S I D E A O A E
V N P A I N F U L N B R D T R
E E D S E C U D O R P D S H D
W E R U O Y L Y F H I S O E L
O B O U R I R A D L E H N R I
H M L E T E T E I N I I W O H
T O U T V H B E S T L P S E C
E R L E E W S U C P L M R S S
T E E R H D O S I E E U E U H
S O S A R E N C P N G C H A O
S V T O T N S E L I I H T C U
E E L H L I V E I L T T A E L
O R G O D A N D N P I I F B D
G I N O T R I G E I M M S T I
R T O H S T P E C C A B H S S
E G P W R E M S A S T U M E C
D V L A E I Y O E I E S N V I
N A E V T S O N P D E I S R P
U H A R N E U T Y H L E E A L
Y H S O Y V H A S P K H U H I
E R A H S O M I I U T T H E N
S O N S U L N C B A H H U O E
O N T G L U S E F O G E M R D
H O H S P I R I T S I M A K E
T T R D D I S C I P L I N E S
```

— — — — — — — — — — — — — — —

— — — discipline, — — — — — —.   Psalm 94:12

A Deadly Weapon

There's probably not a person alive who has not been hurt by cruel words. We all know that the tongue is a deadly weapon. The **apostle** James had quite a bit to say about this weapon:

If **anyone** considers **himself religious** and yet does not keep a **tight rein** on his **tongue**, he **deceives** himself and his **religion** is **worthless**.

James 1:26

When we put **bits** into the **mouths** of **horses** to make them **obey** us, we can turn the **whole animal**. Or take ships as an example. **Although** they are so **large** and are **driven** by **strong** winds, they are steered by a very small rudder wherever the pilot wants to go. **Likewise** the **tongue** is a small part of the **body**, but it makes **great** boasts. **Consider** what a great **forest** is **set** on **fire** by a small spark. The **tongue** also is a **fire**, a world of evil **among** the parts of the **body**. It **corrupts** the **whole person**, sets the whole **course** of his life on **fire**, and is itself **set** on fire by **hell**.

All kinds of animals, birds, reptiles and **creatures** of the **sea** are being tamed and have been tamed by **man**. But no man **can tame** the tongue. It is a restless evil, full of deadly poison.

With the tongue we **praise** our **Lord** and Father, and **with** it we curse **men**, **who** have been made in God's likeness. Out of the same **mouth** come praise and **cursing**. My **brothers**, this **should not** be.

James 3:3-10

```
            E
            S
        T I         G
        O W         N R
        Y N E       I E
M       D G K E     S L S
O       O U I N     R I S R R
U L     B E L O H W U G E E
T A     O H O Y S I C I L D L
H R H D E R N O T N O H I I
S G T Y L D A E H E U T S G
N E U F L E S M I H S R N I
E A O O B E Y E O W H O O O
V T M S H S L C A N R W C N
I H S B I T S R E T G T S S
R G T R S A L E S E L O H W
D I S O A E M A T S C N O
S T P T N R E T F E O G U
C A N H I G N U O S R U L
F I R E M N U R R R R E D
  I P R A I S E E U U R
  R S L E P S S O P I
  S E S R O H T C T F
  D E C E I V E S
```

New Life in Christ

Have you ever been so discouraged and depressed that you wished you could just start your life all over again? No wonder the idea of reincarnation has such appeal! But God **promises** us that no such opportunity **exists**: "**Man** is **destined** to **die once**, and **after** that to **face judgment**" (Hebrews 9:27).

No, God's plan for **new** life involves the life we are now living, with all the tragedies and regrets we have. He **promises** simply (and incredibly) to create a **new** person to replace the old.

"You **were taught**, with **regard** to your **former way** of **life**, to **put** off your **old self**, **which** is **being corrupted** by its **deceitful desires**; to be made **new** in the **attitude** of your **minds**; and to **put** on the **new self**, **created** to be **like God** in **true righteousness** and **holiness**" (Ephesians 4:22-24).

"**Praise** be to the **God** and **Father** of **our Lord Jesus Christ!** In **his great mercy** he **has given** us **new birth into** a **living hope through** the **resurrection** of **Jesus Christ from the dead**" (1 Peter 1:3).

"We **were therefore buried** with **him through baptism** into **death** in **order that**, **just** as **Christ** was **raised** from the **dead** . . . we too may **live** a **new life**" (Romans 6:4).

"**Therefore**, if **anyone** is in **Christ**, he is a **new creation**; the old **has gone**, the new has **come!**" (2 Corinthians 5:17).

You can begin again. Your **sins** can be forgiven, your life can be washed clean. And, with God's Holy Spirit living in you, you need never go back to a sinful life again.

```
I S D N I M T F O R M E R D R F
N E D S U S E J L O R D I E E R
T L D E N I T S E D W R G A H O
O F T A T T I T U D E A H T T M
H T H H O P E E K S R E T H A T
S N R H U A U T U D E W E C F H
S E O T R B U R I E D E O I T E
E M U R H P R H R Y R N U H E D
N G G I S E S I M O R P S W R E
I D H B C W R M F W C P N E W A
L U F T I E C E D E G R E A T D
O J I O W S R R F N D A S B I E
H O R D A E D P R O M I S E S F
N Y E E H R N E W G R S R I G I
A C D T S I R H C E N E W N N L
M R R A I S E D H X W A Y G I S
E E O E S E C H R I S T L I V E
C M N R A D O G I S I H E F I L
A O N C E T H A S T N G O D L F
F E M C H R I S T S S U S E J W
T R U E H G U O R H T A L I K E
W G I V E N O Y N A H T S U J N
```

_ _ _   _ _ _ _   _ _ _ _   _ _   "_ _ _!"

How Does a Christian Act?

The apostle Paul, writing to the churches in Galatia, gave some very clear guidelines regarding things a Christian should, and should not do. The freedom that he refers to is the result of Jesus Christ having replaced the old, strict laws with the law of love, and having paid for our sins with His own death, so that Christians are free from the penalty of sin.

You, my **brothers**, were **called** to be **free**. But do not use your **freedom** to **indulge** the **sinful nature; rather, serve** one **another** in love. The **entire** law is **summed** up in a **single command**: "**Love your neighbor** as **yourself**." If you **keep** on **biting** and **devouring** each **other, watch** out or you will be **destroyed** by **each other**.

So I say, live by the Spirit, and you will not **gratify** the **desires** of the sinful nature. For the **sinful nature desires** what is **contrary** to the Spirit, and the Spirit **what** is **contrary** to the sinful nature. . . .

The acts of the **sinful nature** are **obvious: sexual immorality, impurity** and **debauchery; idolatry** and **witchcraft; hatred, discord, jealousy**, fits of **rage**, selfish **ambition, dissensions, factions** and **envy; drunkenness, orgies**, and the like. I warn you, as I did before, that those who live like this will **not inherit** the **kingdom** of God.

But the **fruit** of the Spirit is **love, joy**, peace, **patience, kindness, goodness**, faithfulness, **gentleness** and **self-control. Against** such **things** there is no law. Those who belong to **Christ Jesus** have **crucified** the **sinful nature** with its **passions** and desires. **Since** we live by the Spirit, let us **keep** in **step** with the Spirit.

Galatians 5:13-25

36

```
F A R O B H G I E N B F T A H W
E R U T A N D E V O U R I N G I
P A S S I O N S S T T E U I R N
W C A L L E D S O H D E R T A H
T I P A T I E N C E E H F D T E
B F T E S N U S B R I L N I I R
E R V C D S U A L U F N I S F I
Y O O O H O U D E S I R E S Y T
L R O T I C S V Y Y C P E E K L
D G D V H L R O R J U L F N D U
E I B E U E U A E W R A S S E F
M O R F S R R A F A C U I I S N
M Y N E S T L S R T E X N O I I
U I V E N O R E I C S E F N R S
S O L O U U H O N H F S U S E J
L F C S O T N I Y R S O L M S T
J O Y Y O S S E N E L T N E G L
S E I G R O K I N G D O M H E O
A M B I T I O N A T U R E G K R
E A C H H E E L G N I S A S I T
E F T O I K P N A T U R E R N N
G R S I N C O M M A N D E E D O
L E I U G T S A N O T H E R N C
U E R R S T R G N I T I B U E F
D D H K E E P A G A I N S T S L
N O C P I Y T I R U P M I A S E
I M M O R A L I T Y V N E N T S
```

_ _ _ _ _ _ _ _ _ _ _ _ _ _   _ _

_ _ _ _   _ _ _   _ _ _ _ _ _ _.

They Only Ask for Money

Why do preachers talk so much about giving? **Because** God **does**! **Sixteen** of Jesus' thirty-eight **parables** are about money **matters**. Jesus **taught more** about the wise use of our **belongings** than about **Heaven** or Hell. He talked about **money** five **times** more often than He talked about **prayer**. Why?

It's **helpful** to **remember** that God **created** us in His own **image**, and He is a very **generous** being! Think about it; He **gave** us **life**, and all the things we need to **sustain** life, and then He **sacrificed** His own **Son** so that our **sins** can be **forgiven** and we can spend **eternity** with Him. Since **God created** us to be like Him, giving is in our nature. We are fully **alive** and our lives have **meaning** when we are **generously helping others**.

The **flip side**, of course, is that we don't feel **good** when we are selfish and **greedy**! **Because God loves** us and wants us to be **happy**, He teaches us about the **dangers** of **loving** money and the **joys** of giving.

"This is how we **know** what love is: **Jesus Christ laid** down his **life** for us. And we **ought** to lay **down** our **lives** for our **brothers**. If **anyone** has **material possessions** and **sees** his **brother** in **need** but has no **pity** on **him**, how can the **love** of God be in him? **Dear children, let** us **not love** with **words** or **tongue** but with **actions** and in **truth. This** then is **how** we know that we **belong** to the **truth**, and how we **set** our **hearts** at **rest** in **his presence whenever** our **hearts condemn** us. For **God** is greater than our **hearts**, and he knows **everything**" (1 John 3:16-20).

```
H O W F J O Y S F R T H G U O
I S T Y T I P O R S R E H T O
S T O E M T R E B E C A U S E
R R N A O G E L V C T R L R A
E A G N I N A E M R E T Y E C
H E U V O I R C H E L S A B T
T H E Y R Y Y H E A V E N M I
O N N E T S N I A T S U S E O
R A T H H I O L R E N U U M N
B A I H I X N D T D O D O E S
M N M P S T A R S R I M O R E
G I E R Y E N E E D S E V O L
H E S E T E R N S T S E E S B
G D N S S N E O G R E E D Y A
G O D E I G S S N I S F V E R
M W D N R O T E I K S I D R A
E N H C H O C D G N O L E B P
G O D E C D U I N O P E C I T
N M E D N O C S O W E V I L A
I V T E D E V O L A I D F O U
V H A F G A V E E Y E O I V G
O T E S U A C E B A R G R E H
L U R L I F E T R U T H C E T
I R C Y P P A H E R E Y A R P
V T L I Y F D A N G E R S G I
E V L J E S U S R E H T O R B
S F E G N I P L E H W O R D S
```

_ _ _ _ _ _   _ _ _   _ _ _ _

_ _ _ _ _ _ _ _   _ _ _ _ _ _ _

_ _ _ _.

Matthew 10:8

The Working Life

Does the Bible have anything to say about how we should work? Yes, God is interested in every aspect of our life.

Make it **your ambition** to **lead** a **quiet life**, to **mind your own business** and to **work** with **your hands, just** as we **told** you, so that your **daily life may win** the **respect** of **outsiders** and so that you will not be **dependent** on **anybody**.

1 Thessalonians 4:11, 12

In the **name** of the **Lord Jesus** Christ, we **command** you, **brothers**, to **keep away** from **every brother** who is **idle** and **does** not **live according** to the **teaching** you **received** from us. . . . We were not **idle** when we were with you, nor **did** we eat **anyone's food without paying** for it. On the **contrary**, we **worked night** and **day, laboring** and **toiling** so that we **would** not be a **burden** to any of you. We did this, . . . in **order** to **make ourselves** a **model** for you to **follow**. For even **when** we were with you, we gave you this **rule:** "If a **man** will not **work**, he **shall** not eat."
We **hear** that some **among** you are **idle**. They are not **busy;** they are **busybodies. Such people** we **command** and **urge** in the **Lord Jesus Christ** to **settle down** and **earn** the **bread** they eat.

2 Thessalonians 3:6-12

Whatever you do, **work** at it with **all** your **heart,** as **working** for the Lord, not for **men, since** you **know** that you **will** receive an **inheritance** from the **Lord** as a **reward**.

Colossians 3:23, 24

```
R D A Y G N I H C A E T E E T
L A B O R I N G O W S Y L D S
N W O U L D Y A M O S O U E I
I P O R S U C H M R O U R V R
G Y W I I Y A W A K R R S I H
H E N C N T B T N E D S T E C
T C N E H W N O D D E E O C J
E G R U E H I U D N R V I E U
L O R D R T W T I I M L L R S
P I E F I L Q S D M E E I O T
O S F B T E U I L H N S N W A
E D M E A B I D E E N R G C N
P A Y I N G E E V A E U C R K
D I D R C H T R I R D O A R R
R L O J E S U S L T R E O L O
A Y W L I V S O R D U W L T W
W N N E D O E S I E B A U H W
E I Y D L L A N O R H O A R Y
R D K O E D G P E S H T M D Y
E L C M N L E A D T E A O H S
S E T T L E D P I V K B N R U
P A F R K D S W E E Y A G M B
E C O N T R A R Y N A M E F O
C L L N H W G H A N D S Y O W
T O L D E O B R O T H E R O I
D R O L A R O C O M M A N D L
U D W O R K I N G M A K E T L
```

_ _ _ _ _ _ _   _ _ _ _ _   _ _ _
_ _ _ _ _   _ _ _ _   _ _ _ _ _   _ _ _.

1 Thessalonians 5:12

The Money Trap

Having money can keep us from trusting God. Why would we need to trust God to provide for us if we could go out and buy whatever we wanted? Solomon, the wisest man who ever lived, realized this when he prayed,

> **Two things** I **ask** of you, O **Lord**; . . .
> **Keep falsehood** and **lies** far from me;
> > **give** me **neither poverty** nor **riches**,
> > but give me **only** my **daily bread**.
>
> **Otherwise**, I **may** have too **much** and **disown** you and **say**, "**Who** is the Lord?"
> Or I may **become poor** and **steal**,
> > and so **dishonor** the **name** of my **God**.

Proverbs 30:7-9

People who want to get **rich fall** into **temptation** and a **trap** and into **many foolish** and **harmful desires** that **plunge men** into **ruin** and **destruction**. For the **love** of **money** is a **root** of all **kinds** of **evil**. **Some people**, **eager** for **money**, have **wandered** from the **faith** and **pierced themselves** with **many griefs**.

Command those who are **rich** in **this present world** not to be **arrogant** nor to **put** their **hope** in **wealth**, which is so **uncertain**, but to **put** their **hope** in **God**, who **richly provides** us with **everything** for our **enjoyment**. **Command them** to do good, to be rich in **good deeds**, and to be **generous** and **willing** to **share**. In this way they will lay up **treasure** for **themselves** as a **firm foundation** for the **coming age**, so that they may take **hold** of the **life** that is **truly** life.

1 Timothy 6:9, 10, 17-19

```
F A L L I V E T U P I E R C E D
I R I C H Y R O O P O T D O M L
R R U N I A T R E C N U E M O R
M O W S U O R E N E G C S M C O
S G E H D A K N M N T B T A E W
D A A T O O R Y O P T R R N B A
N N L N G M O N E Y T E U D M N
I T T E S J W H O S H A C L A T
K L H S N E R A E V S D T W Y F
T O S E H C I R M S I E I I R O
H V B R M E I M A T L E O L O U
I E P P O S T F N E O A N L N N
N M R H E O E U Y A O G F I O D
G A O D G H O L D L F E O N H A
S N V H N T I D V L O R D G S T
E V I G O A D E R E D N A W I I
G O D H D P M U C H S A Y A D O
Y E E A T H E M S E L V E S O N
E L S N S Y S L O H P E S K O E
N P H D D I R I W C O M I N G M
O O E C H O P E T I V O W E R A
M E H T I R L S V R E S R I I N
D P T M E R U S A E R T E T E Y
O D I S O W N I P U T R H H F L
E R A H S A G E N N Y A T E S N
L I F E E P E O P L E P O R Y O
```

__ __ __ __ __ __ __ __ __ __ __ __

__ __ __ __ __ __ __ __ __ __ __ __ __ __ __.

Luke 16:13

Keeping Perspective

Do not be **overawed** when a **man grows rich**,
  when the **splendor** of **his house** increases;
for he will take **nothing** with him when he **dies**,
  his splendor will not **descend** with him.
Though while he lived he **counted** himself **blessed**—
  and men **praise** you when you **prosper**—
he will join the **generation** of **his fathers**,
  who will never see the light of life.
A man who has **riches without understanding**
  is like the **beasts** that **perish**.

Psalm 49:16-20

    Consider how the **lilies grow**. They do not **labor** or **spin**. **Yet** I tell you, not **even Solomon** in all **his splendor** was **dressed** like one of **these**. If that is how **God clothes** the **grass** of the **field**, which is **here** today, and **tomorrow** is **thrown** into the **fire**, how much **more** will he **clothe** you, O you of little **faith**! And do not set your **heart** on what you will eat or **drink**; do not **worry about** it. For the **pagan world runs** after all **such things**, and **your Father knows** that you **need** them. But **seek** his **kingdom**, and these **things** will be **given** to you as well.

    Do not be **afraid**, little **flock**, for your **Father** has **been pleased** to give you the kingdom. **Sell** your **possessions** and give to the **poor**. **Provide purses** for **yourselves** that will not **wear out**, a **treasure** in **heaven** that will not be **exhausted**, **where** no **thief** comes near and no **moth destroys**. For **where** your **treasure** is, there your **heart** will be **also**.

Luke 12:27-34

```
M A N E E D G N W O R H T F W E
S E I L I L O H S I R E P I E H
D N E C S E D S E S S R T R R T
E P G S H I A E I L T E R E O O
W F R W O F P H D E S S E R D L
A A A O U T U T H P A G A N N C
R T S R S G R O W G E N S E E F
E H S G E P S L H N B I U V L A
V E T H E S E C E I I H R I P T
O R X H C U S R P D S T E G S H
S S W H F O A F R N R W H E R E
B T T G A T H E O A L E T S F R
L P H U I U S I V T M N A I L O
E R I O T O S H I S O O F T O B
S A N H H S R T D R T M R R C A
S I G T E L U N E E H O A E K L
E S S T A O H E D D L I A D L
D E S T R O Y S T N A O D S Y E
N O T H I N G O E U F S R U N S
P L E A S E D L Y W H E A R T P
R H E D E S P L E N D O R E O I
S E V L E S R U O Y R I C H M N
W A E R K N E V A E H Y R R O W
O R N O A N E E B S E H C I R H
N T T W E A R C O N S I D E R E
K N I R D E T N U O C S P O O R
M O D G N I K H T U O H T I W E
```

_ _ _ _ _ _ _ _ _ _ _ _ _ _ _ _

_ _ _ _ _ _ _ _ _ _ _ _ _ _ _.

Proverbs 11:4

Is God a Wimp?

"If God is the loving **father** of us all," some argue, "how can He send anyone to Hell?" God has promised to forgive (and forget) our sins IF we believe that He **sent** His **son** Jesus to **die** to pay the **penalty** for our **sins** and IF we **accept Jesus** as our Savior, thereby accepting the **gift** of God's **grace.** (Grace is God's **unearned loving kindness** toward us.) Jesus said, "For my **Father's** will is **that** everyone who **looks** to the **Son** and **believes** in him **shall have eternal life**" (John 6:40).

Those who have not accepted **Jesus** as their personal Savior are now **enjoying** God's **patience,** but they are "living on **borrowed** time." The apostle Peter said, "The Lord is not **slow** in **keeping** his **promise.** . . . He is **patient** with you, not **wanting** anyone to **perish,** but everyone to **come** to **repentance.**" Peter's next **sentence** was this: "But the **day** of the **Lord will come** like a **thief**" (2 Peter 3:9, 10). Meaning we will not know when it is going to happen.

"We will all **stand before God's judgment seat,**" Paul **wrote** in his **letter** to the **Christians** in Rome. And then he quoted the Lord: "'As **surely** as I **live**' says the **Lord,** '**every knee will bow before** me; **every tongue** will **confess** to God.'"

"So then," (continued Paul) "**each** of us will **give** an **account** of **himself** to God" (Romans 14:10-12).

"Do **not** be **deceived: God cannot** be **mocked.** A man **reaps** what he **sows.** The **one who sows** to **please** his **sinful nature,** from that **nature** will **reap destruction;** the **one** who **sows** to **please** the **Spirit,** from the **Spirit** will **reap eternal life**" (Galatians 6:7, 8).

```
S O W S P E C N E T N E S S T
B N H A R M O C K E D C E O E
E E E O W N G N I T N A W E
F R P R M E R O F E B A T S M
O G E U I T N O S O R T A T O
R N N T S E T S W T O N N A C
E I A A E R E H T A F E H E H
G P L N N N T W N T M P G V R
N E T O D A Y O I G L E O I I
I E Y N H L T R D L O R D G S
Y K I T F G I U A I L O S N T
O K R E A P J H R F W H O I I
J E S U S D S I F E I H T V A
N D E C E I V E D M S N C O N
E G L S V S O W S N U W O L S
E O U E E T P E C O R H M O H
V D F M I T L I C I E S E E A
I I N R L F E C N T L I G C V
L L I W E I A C E C Y R C A E
O P S L B G S P S U S E J R D
S O T S Y S E E A R P P S G E
R S O S R I A T E T O R W O W
E K N E E D I E L S I N S D O
H O G F V N D R P E V E R Y R
T O U N E A R N E D S E N T R
A L E O N T O A S P A E R T O
F E A C H S L L E T T E R S B
```

__ __ __ __ __ __ __ __ __ __ __ __ __ __ __

__ __ __ __ __ __. __ __ __ __ __ __ __ __ __ __ __ 3:6

A Time for Everything

There is a **time** for **everything,**
and a **season** for **every activity under** heaven:
A time to be **born** and a time to **die,**
a time to **plant** and a time to **uproot,**
a time to **kill** and a time to **heal,**
a time to **tear down** and a time to **build,**
a time to **weep** and a time to **laugh,**
a time to **mourn** and a time to **dance,**
a time to **scatter stones** and a time to **gather them,**
a time to **embrace** and a time to **refrain,**
a time to **search** and a time to **give up,**
a time to **keep** and a time to **throw away,**
a time to **tear** and a time to **mend,**
a time to be **silent** and a time to **speak,**
a time to **love** and a time to **hate,**
a time for **war** and a time for **peace.**

```
            N W O D
          T I M E L R I E
        T C N E V A E H E K
      B O R N E E U D D T G I
    D C O A L C R G N L N E N L
  T N S R E S N Y H U I A S I I L
  H E P P T G A A Y H U L I A P A
  R M E U H A D S T E B P L R E E
  O E A T E T N Y I M H S E F A H
W H K L R H R A V B A T N E C T
  T U O E E U W I R T O T R E
    P V V R O A T A E N A A
      E I E M R C C S E R
        G N O S A E S S
            P E E K
```

— — — — — — — — — — — 3:1-8